English - Arabic

Vocabulary building is crucial for children as it improves communication skills, comprehension and academic success. This is a gradual process and using this book can be a great starting point for your children.

To build vocabulary, read together, play word games, practice with flashcards, encourage writing, use words in daily life, review regularly. It is essential to be patient and persistent with your child as he learns new words.

To watch the video alongside this book, simply go to the website provided on the last page. You can freely access it as per your convenience. Let's start!

whale

حوت

SUBSCRIBE

Lifetime Access !!!

#1 bee  نحلة	#2 hawk  صقر	#3 walrus  فظ
#4 moth  عثة	#5 puppy  جرو	#6 ostrich  نعامة
#7 horse  حصان	#8 hen  دجاجة	#9 turkey  ديك رومي

#10
eagle

نسر

#11
camel

جمل

#12
porcupine

نيص

#13
cockroach

صرصور

#14
squirrel

سنجاب

#15
swan

بجعة

#16
stork

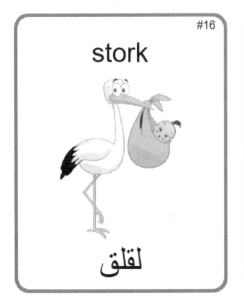

لقلق

#17
fox

ثعلب

#18
wasp

دبور

#19
fish

سمكة

#20
mole

الخلد

#21
reindeer

رنة

#22
mouse

فأر

#23
chicken

دجاجة

#24
duck

بطة

#25
pigeon

حمامة

#26
starfish

نجم البحر

#27
worm

دودة

#28
shark

قرش

#29
mare

فرس

#30
butterfly

فراشة

#31
goose

أوزة

#32
crow

غراب

#33
monkey

قرد

#34
toad

علجوم

#35
mermaid

حورية البحر

#36
whale

حوت

#37
caterpillar

يرقة

#38
peacock

طاووس

#39
centipede

أم أربع وأربعين

#40
ant

نملة

#41
lobster

سرطان البحر

#42
unicorn

وحيد القرن

#43
lion

أسد

#44
hippopotamus

فرس النهر

#45
rooster

ديك

#46
seagull

نورس

#47
kitten

قط صغير

#48
cow

بقرة

#49
rabbit

أرنب

#50
jellyfish

قنديل البحر

#51
dog

كلب

#52
vulture

نسر

#53
squid

حبار

#54
snail

حلزون

#55	#56	#57
parrot	insect	monster

ببغاء	حشرة	وحش

#58	#59	#60
crab	dove	mice

سلطعون	حمامة	فئران

#61	#62	#63
rat	goat	cheetah

جرذ	ماعز	فهد

#64
elephant

فيل

#65
grasshopper

جرادة

#66
bird

طائر

#67
quail

طائر السمان

#68
owl

بومة

#69
dolphin

دلفين

#70
frog

ضفدع

#71
cat

قطة

#72
boar

خنزير بري

#73
mosquito

بعوضة

#74
pelican

بجع

#75
turtle

سلحفاة

#76
ladybug

خنفساء صغيرة

#77
deer

أيل

#78
octopus

أخطبوط

#79
tiger

نمر

#80
clam

محار

#81
hedgehog

قنفذ

#82
sheep

خروف

#83
kangaroo

كنغر

#84
alligator

تمساح

#85
lizard

سحلية

#86
spider

عنكبوت

#87
dinosaur

ديناصور

#88
animal

حيوان

#89
beetle

خنفساء

#90
oyster

محار

#91
sparrow

عصفور

#92
snake

ثعبان

#93
pig

خنزير

#94
dragonfly

يعسوب

#95
helicopter

مروحية

#96
plane

طائرة

#97
vehicle

مركبة

#98
scooter

سكوتر

#99
parachute

مظلة

#100
motorcycle

دراجة نارية

#101
bicycle

دراجة

#102
sailboat

مركب شراعي

#103
boat

قارب

#104
airplane

طائرة

#105
truck

شاحنة

#106
train

قطار

#107
rocket

صاروخ

#108
ship

سفينة

#109
ferry

عبّارة

#110
wagon

عربة

#111
car

سيارة

#112
barrow

عربة يد

#113
submarine

غواصة

#114
subway
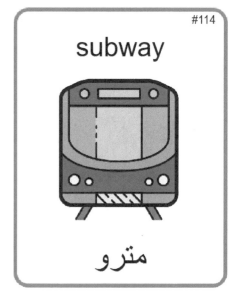
مترو

#115
stomach

بطن

#116
muscle

عضلة

#117
eyebrows

حواجب

#118

neck

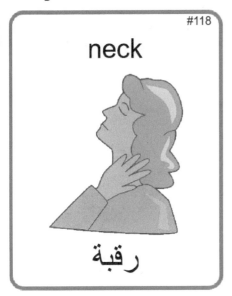

رقبة

#119

bone

عظم

#120

elbow

مِرفَق

#121

hips

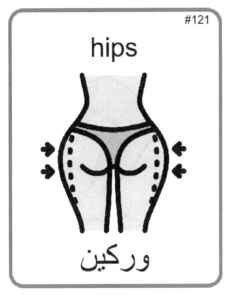

وركين

#122

waist

خصر

#123

hair

شعر

#124

tongue

لسان

#125

hands

يدين

#126

shoulder

كتف

#127
legs

أرجل

#128
chest
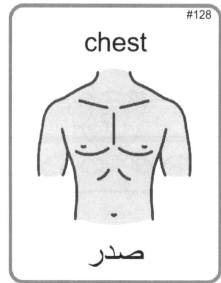
صدر

#129
forehead
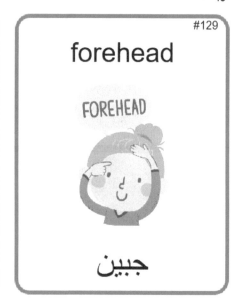
جبين

#130
wing

جناح

#131
teeth
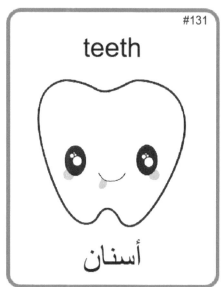
أسنان

#132
leg
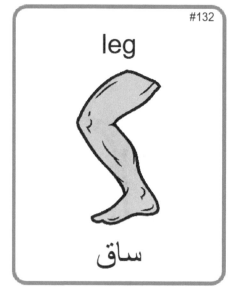
ساق

#133
brain

دماغ

#134
thumb

إبهام

#135
tail

ذيل

#136
chin
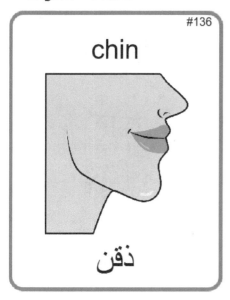
ذقن

#137
nose

أنف

#138
fin

زعنفة

#139
knees

ركبتين

#140
face

وجه

#141
foot

قدم

#142
feet

أقدام

#143
lips
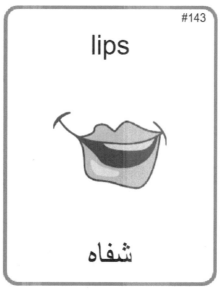
شفاه

#144
mouth
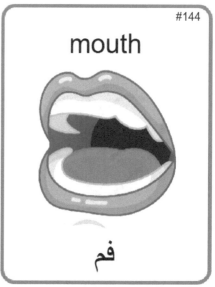
فم

#145
blood
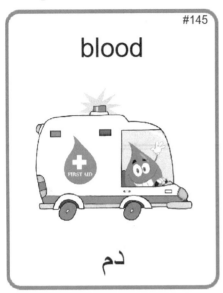
دم

#146
wig

شعر مستعار

#147
beard

لحية

#148
hip
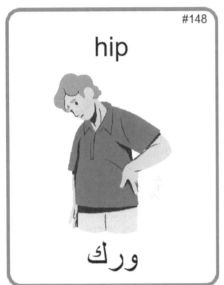
ورك

#149
glue

صمغ

#150
throat
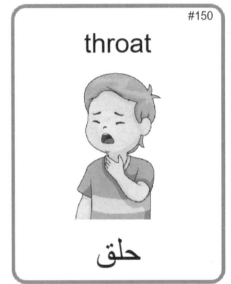
حلق

#151
heart

قلب

#152
toes

أصابع القدم

#153
shoulders

أكتاف

#154
cheeks

خدود

#155
body

جسم

#156
head

رأس

#157
tooth

سن

#158
ear
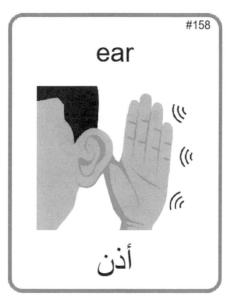
أذن

#159
eye
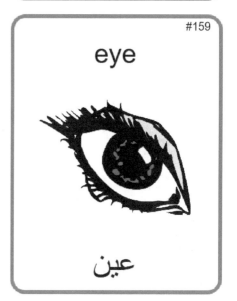
عين

#160
football

كرة القدم

#161
surfing

ركوب الأمواج

#162
cycling

ركوب الدراجات

#163
fishing

صيد السمك

#164
jogging

هرولة

#165
racket

مضرب

#166
dance

رقص

#167
soccer

كرة القدم

#168
kite

طائرة ورقية

#169
ride

ركوب

#170
driving

قيادة

#171
swimming

سباحة

#172
fight

قتال

#173
team

فريق

#174
wrestling

مصارعة

#175
boxing

ملاكمة

#176
hopping

قفز

#177
archery

رماية

#178
gymnastics

جمباز

#179
climbing

تسلق

#180
dive

غطس

#181
timer

مؤقت

#182
dumbbells

أثقال

#183
sunday

الأحد

#184
saturday

السبت

#185
friday

الجمعة

#186
thursday

الخميس

#187
monday

الاثنين

#188
tuesday

الثلاثاء

#189
wednesday

الأربعاء

#190
receptionist

موظف استقبال

#191
driver

سائق

#192
army

جيش

#193
leader

قائد

#194
secretary

سكرتير

#195
policeman

شرطي

#196
actor

ممثل

#197
cashier

أمين الصندوق

#198
bishop

أسقف

#199

pharmacist

صيدلي

#200

butcher

جزار

#201

veterinarian

طبيب بيطري

#202

magician

الساحر

#203

knight

فارس

#204

maid

خادمة

#205

queen

ملكة

#206

farmer

مزارع

#207

princess

أميرة

#208

bartender

نادل

#209

politician

سياسي

#210

waiter

نادل

#211

judge

قاضي

#212

nurse

ممرضة

#213

carpenter

نجار

#214

barber

حلاق

#215

lawyer

محام

#216

miner

عامل منجم

#217
ghost

شبح

#218
entrepreneur

رائد أعمال

#219
teacher

معلم

#220
singer

مغني

#221
pirate

قرصان

#222
accountant

محاسب

#223
baker

خباز

#224
police

شرطة

#225
fisherman

صياد السمك

#226
optician

أخصائي بصريات

#227
president

رئيس

#228
plumber

سباك

#229
cop

شرطي

#230
photographer
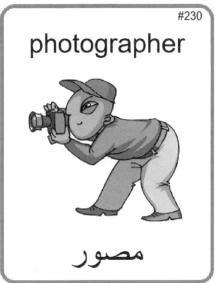
مصور

#231
boss

رئيس

#232
king

ملك

#233
doctor

طبيب

#234
witch

ساحرة

#235

writer

كاتب

#236

hairdresser

حلاق

#237

angel

ملاك

#238

artist

فنان

#239

chef

طاه

#240

musician

موسيقي

#241

florist

بائع الزهور

#242

white

color the word and
the picture in pink

white

أبيض

#243

gray

color the word and
the picture in pink

gray

رمادي

#244
red

أحمر

#245
blue

color the word and
the picture in pink
أزرق

#246
brown

color the word and
the picture in pink
بني

#247
green

color the word and
the picture in pink
أخضر

#248
pink
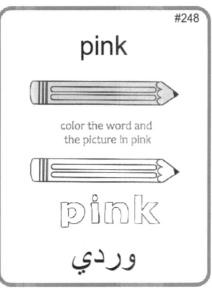
color the word and
the picture in pink
وردي

#249
yellow

color the word and
the picture in pink
أصفر

#250
child

طفل

#251
granddaughter

حفيدة

#252
man

رجل

#253
family

عائلة

#254
stepdaughter

ابنة زوج

#255
kids

أطفال

#256
father

أب

#257
uncle

عم

#258
dad

أب

#259
girl

فتاة

#260
toddler

طفل صغير

#261
niece

ابنة الأخ

#262
woman

امرأة

#263
kid

طفل

#264
mother

أم

#265
boy

ولد

#266
brother

أخ

#267
people

الناس

#268
children

أطفال

#269
cousin

ابن عم

#270
member

عضو

#271

aunt

عمة

#272

son

ابن

#273

group

مجموعة

#274

girlfriend

صديقة

#275

daughter

ابنة

#276

grandmother

جدة

#277

grandson

حفيد

#278

boyfriend

حبيب

#279

lady

سيدة

#280

wife

زوجة

#281

friend

صديق

#282

nephew

ابن الأخ

#283

sister

أخت

#284

stepmother

زوجة الأب

#285

stepson

ابن زوج

#286

mom

أم

#287

cabinet

خزانة

#288

pants

بنطال

#289
lightbulb

مصباح

#290
pacifier

لهاية

#291
cap

قبعة

#292
crayons

ألوان شمعية

#293
telescope

تلسكوب

#294
refrigerator
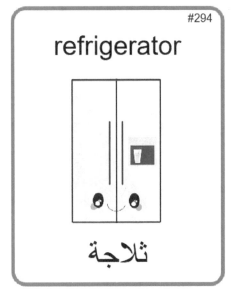
ثلاجة

#295
saucer

صحن صغير

#296
tent

خيمة

#297
strainer
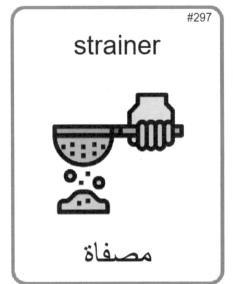
مصفاة

#298
bin

سلة قمامة

#299
pearls

لؤلؤ

#300
bucket

دلو

#301
oil

زيت

#302
vest

سترة بدون أكمام

#303
cup

كوب

#304
gasoline

بنزين

#305
rope

حبل

#306
knife

سكين

#307
scarf

وشاح

#308
gift

هدية

#309
typewriter

آلة كاتبة

#310
fan
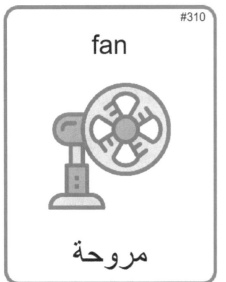
مروحة

#311
vaccine

لقاح

#312
hat

قبعة

#313
basket

سلة

#314
flag

علم

#315
coat

معطف

#316	#317	#318
helmet	bouquet	compass

خوذة	باقة	بوصلة

#319	#320	#321
money	toy	earring
		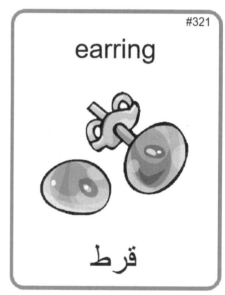
مال	لعبة	قرط

#322	#323	#324
yarn	machine	bag

خيط	آلة	حقيبة

#325
carpet

سجادة

#326
hanger

علاقة ملابس

#327
kettle

غلاية

#328
bowl

وعاء

#329
pitcher

إبريق

#330
pencil

قلم رصاص

#331
glass

زجاج

#332
lantern

فانوس

#333
paper

ورقة

#334
device

جهاز

#335
cage

قفص

#336
cleanser

منظف

#337
notebook

دفتر

#338
undershirt

قميص داخلي

#339
backpack

حقيبة ظهر

#340
blanket

بطانية

#341
underpants

ملابس داخلية

#342
magazine

مجلة

#343
screwdriver

مفك براغي

#344
stapler

دباسة

#345
rake

مدمة

#346
wrench

مفتاح ربط

#347
bracelet

سوار

#348
letter

رسالة

#349
wood

خشب

#350
handkerchief

منديل

#351
pan

مقلاة

#352
jacket

سترة

#353
umbrella

مظلة

#354
bedroom

غرفة نوم

#355
clothes

ملابس

#356
table

طاولة

#357
toothpaste
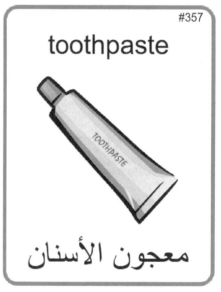
معجون الأسنان

#358
lipstick

أحمر شفاه

#359
comb
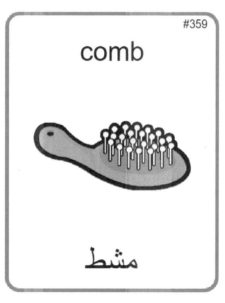
مشط

#360
barrel

برميل

#361

pajamas

بيجامة

#362

clock

ساعة

#363

chair

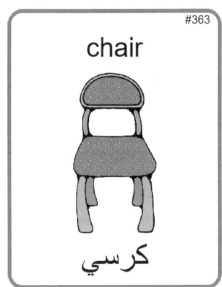

كرسي

#364

collar

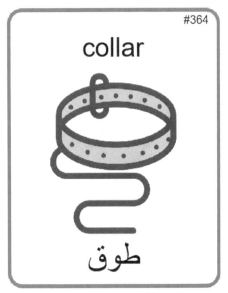

طوق

#365

brush

فرشاة

#366

broom

مكنسة

#367

bassinet

مهد

#368

diamond

ألماس

#369

microscope

مجهر

#370
television

تلفاز

#371
lamp

مصباح

#372
toothbrush

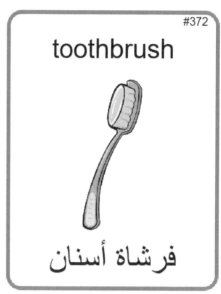

فرشاة أسنان

#373
engine

محرك

#374
window

نافذة

#375
silk

حرير

#376
bookcase

خزانة كتب

#377
pin

دبوس

#378
bookshelf

رف كتب

#379
cash

نقد

#380
skirt

تنورة

#381
bottle

زجاجة

#382
eraser

ممحاة

#383
mug

قدح

#384
suitcase

حقيبة سفر

#385
trousers

سروال

#386
belt

حزام

#387
metal

معدن

#388
wallet

محفظة

#389
razor

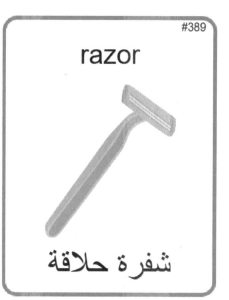

شفرة حلاقة

#390
spatula

ملعقة مسطحة

#391
toilet

مرحاض

#392
towel

منشفة

#393
pot

قدر

#394
wreath

إكليل الزهور

#395
cupboard

خزانة الصحون

#396
chainsaw

منشار كهربائي

#397
cushion

وسادة

#398
prize

جائزة

#399
pillow

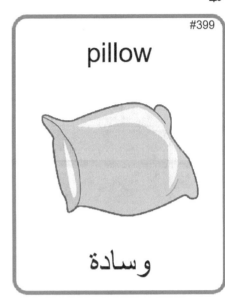

وسادة

#400
stockings

جوارب طويلة

#401
ruler

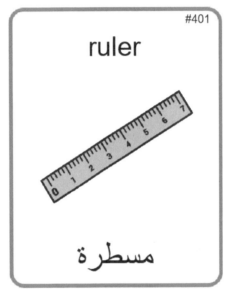

مسطرة

#402
mirror

مرآة

#403
apron

مئزر

#404
plate

طبق

#405
tray

صينية

#406
spoon

ملعقة

#407
dish

طبق

#408
pen

قلم

#409
ladder

سلم

#410
phone

هاتف

#411
teapot

إبريق شاي

#412
alcohol

كحول

#413
fireplace

مدفأة

#414
newspaper

صحيفة

#415
oven

فرن

#416
ink

حبر

#417
cactus
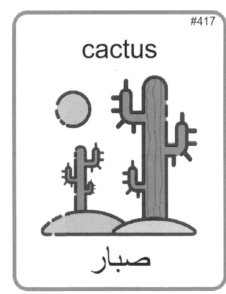
صبار

#418
tire

إطار

#419
book

كتاب

#420
seeds

بذور

#421
calculator

آلة حاسبة

#422
necklace
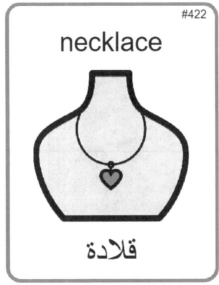
قلادة

#423
glove

قفاز

#424
shirt

قميص

#425
telephone

هاتف

#426
mask

قناع

#427
microphone

ميكروفون

#428
socks

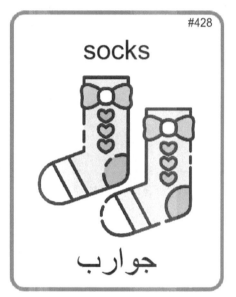

جوارب

#429
kitchen

مطبخ

#430
map

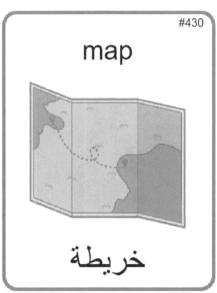

خريطة

#431
shoes

أحذية

#432
rug

سجادة

#433

soap

صابون

#434

photo

صورة

#435

lid

غطاء

#436

raincoat

معطف مطر

#437

dictionary

قاموس

#438

closet

خزانة

#439

dress

فستان

#440

bathtub

حوض استحمام

#441

pliers

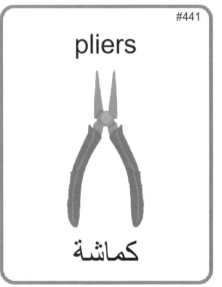

كماشة

#442
bell
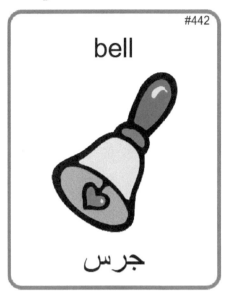
جرس

#443
bowtie

ربطة عنق

#444
torch

شعلة

#445
sweater

كنزة

#446
picture

صورة

#447
bed

سرير

#448
chalkboard

سبورة

#449
syringe
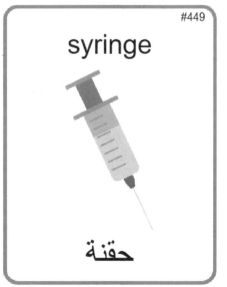
حقنة

#450
calendar

تقويم

#451
fork

شوكة

#452
paintbrush

فرشاة رسم

#453
key

مفتاح

#454
jug

إبريق

#455
napkin

منديل

#456
camera

كاميرا

#457
stove

موقد

#458
dice

نرد

#459
tool

أداة

#460
shorts

سروال قصير

#461
teacup

فنجان شاي

#462
box

صندوق

#463
doll

دمية

#464
scissors

مقص

#465
desk

مكتب

#466
mat

حصيرة

#467
diaper

حفاضة

#468
equipment

معدات

#469
candle

شمعة

#470
cot

سرير أطفال

#471
crayon

قلم تلوين

#472
curtains
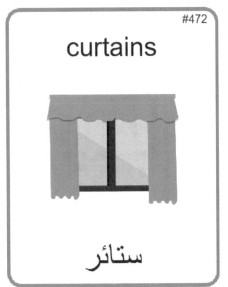
ستائر

#473
slippers
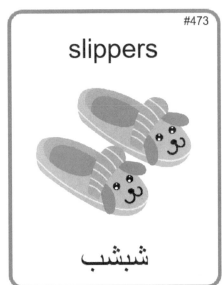
شبشب

#474
utensils

أدوات مطبخ

#475
bomb

قنبلة

#476
gun

مسدس

#477
boot

حذاء

#478

shovel

مجرفة

#479

ax

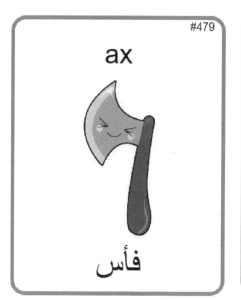

فأس

#480

briefcase

حقيبة مستندات

#481

house

منزل

#482

flower

زهرة

#483

hut

كوخ

#484

wall

جدار

#485

fence

سياج

#486

pool

بركة

#487

gate

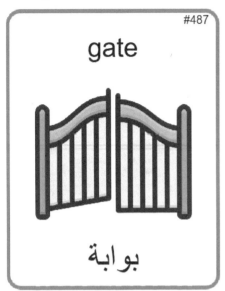

بوابة

#488

area

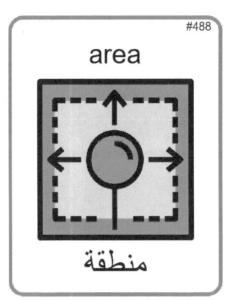

منطقة

#489

soil

تربة

#490

dust

غبار

#491

field

حقل

#492

leaf

ورقة شجر

#493

trash

قمامة

#494

gravel

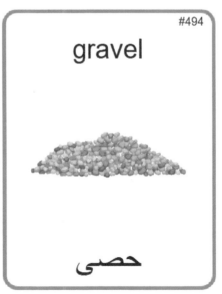

حصى

#495

sinks

أحواض

#496
garbage

قمامة

#497
clothesline

حبل غسيل

#498
home

منزل

#499
grass
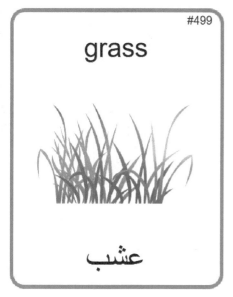
عشب

#500
office

مكتب

#501
stone

حجر

#502
farm

مزرعة

#503
faucet

حنفية

#504
pipe
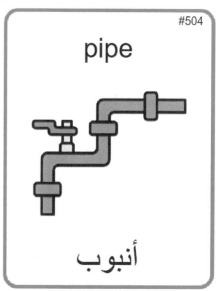
أنبوب

#505
street

شارع

#506
tree

شجرة

#507
puddle

بركة

#508
ground

أرض

#509
chimney

مدخنة

#510
bridge

جسر

#511
curtain

ستارة

#512
roof

سقف

#513
building

مبنى

#514
tombstone

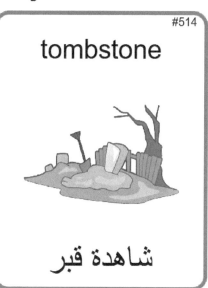

شاهدة قبر

#515
palm

نخلة

#516
mud

طين

#517
road

طريق

#518
windmill

طاحونة هوائية

#519
bathroom

حمام

#520
shower

دش

#521
garden

حديقة

#522
shelter

ملجأ

#523
castle

قلعة

#524
brick

طوب

#525
hall

قاعة

#526
room

غرفة

#527
rock

صخرة

#528
door

باب

#529
wag

هز

#530
close

أغلق

#531
speak

يتكلم

#532
enjoy

استمتع

#533
choose

اختار

#534
open

فتح

#535
snore

شخير

#536
sick

مريض

#537
solve

حل

#538
grow

نمى

#539
read

يقرأ

#540
smile

ابتسامة

#541
sketch

رسم تخطيطي

#542
rob

سرقة

#543
nap

قيلولة

#544
hello

مرحبا

#545
cry

بكى

#546
laugh

ضحك

#547
roast

شوى

#548
hug

عناق

#549
help

يساعد

#550
clap

صفق

#551
discuss

يناقش

#552
kiss

قبلة

#553
nibble

قضم

#554
prepare

تحضير

#555
sleep

نوم

#556
wait

انتظر

#557
decrease
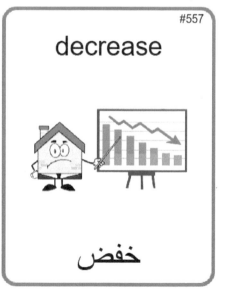
خفض

#558
smell

رائحة

#559
drill

مثقاب

#560
cook

طبخ

#561
love

حب

#562
thank

شكر

#563
clean

نظف

#564
give

أعطى

#565
climb

تسلق

#566
create

أنشأ

#567
hurt

يؤذي

#568
achieve

حقق

#569
knit

حياكة

#570
respect

احترام

#571
protect

يحمي

#572
discover

اكتشف

#573
buy

اشترى

#574
run

ركض

#575
talk

تحدث

#576
think

فكر

#577	#578	#579
eat	celebrate	cut

أكل	احتفل	قطع

#580	#581	#582
grill	crawl	tame

شوى	زحف	ترويض

#583	#584	#585
improve	prevent	bake

يحسن	منع	خبز

#586
remember

تذكر

#587
sing

غنى

#588
receive
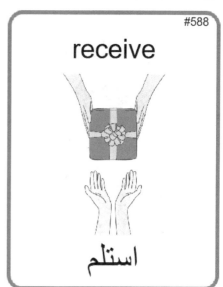
استلم

#589
beg

توسل

#590
build

بناء

#591
walk

مشى

#592
teach

تدريس

#593
understand

فهم

#594
listen

استمع

#595

goodbye

وداعا

#596

dream

حلم

#597

hide

اختباء

#598

dig

يحفر

#599

meet

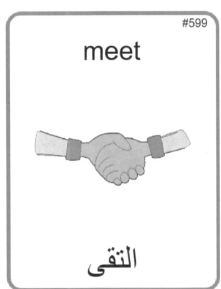

التقى

#600

sew

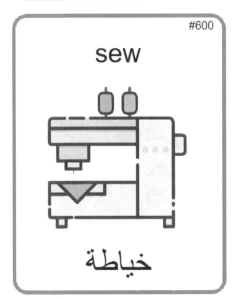

خياطة

#601

play

يلعب

#602

prefer

يفضل

#603

fry

يقلى

#604

follow

يتبع

#605

drink

شرب

#606

sit

يجلس

#607

stop

قف

#608

forbid

منع

#609

bite

يعض

#610

jump

قفز

#611

race

سباق

#612

angry

غاضب

#613 **shake**  هز	#614 **bathe**  استحم	#615 **avoid**  يتجنب
#616 **fly**  طيران	#617 **believe**  صدق	#618 **wash**  غسل
#619 **develop**  تطوير	#620 **win**  فاز	#621 **come**  تعال

#622
write

اكتب

#623
invest

استثمر

#624
boil

غلى

#625
piano

بيانو

#626
music

موسيقى

#627
guitar

غيتار

#628
violin

كمان

#629
drum

طبلة

#630
zero

صفر

#631
one

واحد

#632
two

اثنان

#633
three

ثلاثة

#634
four

أربعة

#635
five

خمسة

#636
six

ستة

#637
seven

سبعة

#638
eight

ثمانية

#639
nine

تسعة

#640
ten

عشرة

#641
eleven

أحد عشر

#642
twelve

اثنا عشر

#643
thirteen

ثلاثة عشر

#644
fourteen

أربعة عشر

#645
fifteen

خمسة عشر

#646
sixteen

ستة عشر

#647
seventeen

سبعة عشر

#648
eighteen

ثمانية عشر

#649
nineteen

تسعة عشر

#650
twenty

عشرون

#651
twenty one

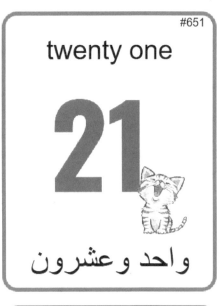

واحد وعشرون

#652
twenty two

22

اثنان وعشرون

#653
twenty three

ثلاثة وعشرون

#654
twenty four

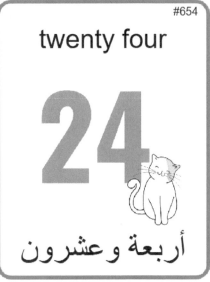

أربعة وعشرون

#655
twenty five

25

خمسة وعشرون

#656
twenty six

ستة وعشرون

#657
twenty seven

سبعة وعشرون

#658

twenty eight

28

ثمانية وعشرون

#659

twenty nine

29

تسعة وعشرون

#660

thirty

30

ثلاثون

#661

thirty one

31

واحد وثلاثون

#662

thirty two

32

اثنان وثلاثون

#663

thirty three

33

ثلاثة وثلاثون

#664

thirty four

34

أربعة وثلاثون

#665

thirty five

35

خمسة وثلاثون

#666

thirty six

36

ستة وثلاثون

#667 thirty seven	#668 thirty eight	#669 thirty nine
37	38	39
سبعة وثلاثون	ثمانية وثلاثون	تسعة وثلاثون

#670 forty	#671 forty one	#672 forty two
40	41	42
أربعون	واحد وأربعون	اثنان وأربعون

#673 forty three	#674 forty four	#675 forty five
43	44	45
ثلاثة وأربعون	أربعة وأربعون	خمسة وأربعون

#676
forty six

46

ستة وأربعون

#677
forty seven

47

سبعة وأربعون

#678
forty eight

48

ثمانية وأربعون

#679
forty nine

49

تسعة وأربعون

#680
fifty

50

خمسون

#681
fifty one

51

واحد وخمسون

#682
fifty two

52

اثنان وخمسون

#683
fifty three

53

ثلاثة وخمسون

#684
fifty four

54

أربعة وخمسون

#685	#686	#687
fifty five	fifty six	fifty seven
55	56	57
خمسة وخمسون	ستة وخمسون	سبعة وخمسون

#688	#689	#690
fifty eight	fifty nine	sixty
58	59	60
ثمانية وخمسون	تسعة وخمسون	ستون

#691	#692	#693
sixty one	sixty two	sixty three
61	62	63
واحد وستون	اثنان وستون	ثلاثة وستون

#694
sixty four

64

أربعة وستون

#695
sixty five

65

خمسة وستون

#696
sixty six

66

ستة وستون

#697
sixty seven

67

سبعة وستون

#698
sixty eight

68

ثمانية وستون

#699
sixty nine

69

تسعة وستون

#700
seventy

70

سبعون

#701
seventy one

71

واحد وسبعون

#702
seventy two

72

اثنان وسبعون

#703
seventy three

73

ثلاثة وسبعون

#704
seventy four

74

أربعة وسبعون

#705
seventy five

75

خمسة وسبعون

#706
seventy six

76

ستة وسبعون

#707
seventy seven

77

سبعة وسبعون

#708
seventy eight

78

ثمانية وسبعون

#709
seventy nine

79

تسعة وسبعون

#710
eighty

80

ثمانون

#711
eighty one

81

واحد وثمانون

#712
eighty two

82

اثنان وثمانون

#713
eighty three

83

ثلاثة وثمانون

#714
eighty four

84

أربعة وثمانون

#715
eighty five

85

خمسة وثمانون

#716
eighty six

86

ستة وثمانون

#717
eighty seven

87

سبعة وثمانون

#718
eighty eight

88

ثمانية وثمانون

#719
eighty nine

89

تسعة وثمانون

#720
ninety

90

تسعون

#721
ninety one
91
واحد وتسعون

#722
ninety two
92
اثنان وتسعون

#723
ninety three
93
ثلاثة وتسعون

#724
ninety four
94
أربعة وتسعون

#725
ninety five
95
خمسة وتسعون

#726
ninety six
96
ستة وتسعون

#727
ninety seven
97
سبعة وتسعون

#728
ninety eight
98
ثمانية وتسعون

#729
ninety nine
99
تسعة وتسعون

#730
hundred

مئة

#731
thousand

ألف

#732
tomato

طماطم

#733
grape
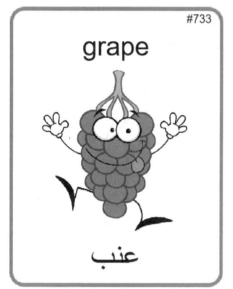
عنب

#734
coffee

قهوة

#735
milk

حليب

#736
cheese

جبن

#737
meat

لحم

#738
apple

تفاحة

#739
lemonade

ليموناضة

#740
plum

برقوق

#741
spinach

سبانخ

#742
radish

فجل

#743
banana

موز

#744
garlic

ثوم

#745
lettuce

خس

#746
shrimp

روبيان

#747
food

طعام

#748
pineapple

أناناس

#749
dinner

عشاء

#750
pepper

فلفل

#751
medicine

دواء

#752
beer

بيرة

#753
celery

كرفس

#754
mushroom

فطر

#755
pie

فطيرة

#756
pomegranate

رمان

#757

turnip

لفت

#758

corn

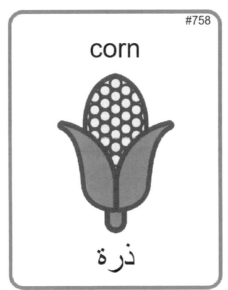

ذرة

#759

cucumber

خيار

#760

apricot

مشمش

#761

eggplant

باذنجان

#762

jam

مربى

#763

chocolate

شوكولاتة

#764

tangerine

يوسفي

#765

soup

حساء

#766	#767	#768
egg	sausage	noodles

بيضة	نقانق	نودلز

#769	#770	#771
breakfast	bean	candy

فطور	فول	حلوى

#772	#773	#774
seafood	sunflower	peas

مأكولات بحرية	زهرة دوار الشمس	بازلاء

#775
cookie

بسكويت

#776
cabbage

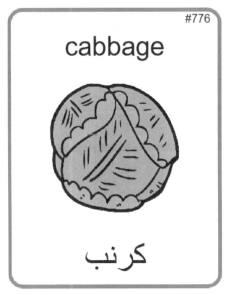

كرنب

#777
cauliflower

قرنبيط

#778
wine

نبيذ

#779
strawberry

فراولة

#780
salt

ملح

#781
honey

عسل

#782
cake

كعكة

#783
popsicles

مثلجات

#784
vegetable

خضروات

#785
potato

بطاطا

#786
peanut

فول سوداني

#787
tea

شاي

#788
meal

وجبة

#789
wheat

قمح

#790
broccoli

بروكلي

#791
carrot

جزر

#792
fruit

فاكهة

#793
salad

سلطة

#794
juice

عصير

#795
bread

خبز

#796
peach

خوخ

#797
lychee

ليتشي

#798
lime

ليم

#799
ham

لحم خنزير

#800
yogurt

زبادي

#801
lemon

ليمون

#802
pear

كمثرى

#803
sugar

سكر

#804
coconut

جوز الهند

#805
pumpkin

يقطين

#806
rice

أرز

#807
water

ماء

#808
raspberry

توت العليق

#809
asparagus

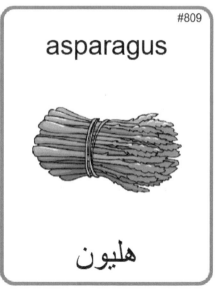

هليون

#810
watermelon

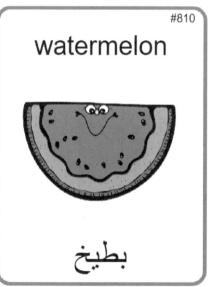

بطيخ

#811
icecream

آيس كريم

#812
tuna

تونة

#813
onion

بصل

#814
lake

بحيرة

#815
snowflake

ندف الثلج

#816
mountain

جبل

#817
river

نهر

#818
atmosphere

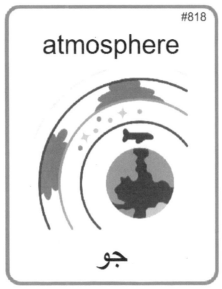

جو

#819
nature

طبيعة

#820
cold

بارد

#821
humid

رطب

#822
world

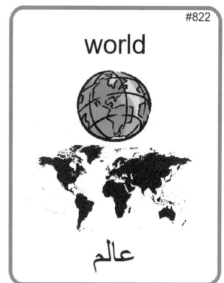

عالم

#823
sun

شمس

#824
heat

حرارة

#825
coast

ساحل

#826
smoke

دخان

#827
star

نجم

#828
windy

عاصف

#829
thunder

رعد

#830
temperature

درجة الحرارة

#831
snowy

مثلج

#832
sound

صوت

#833
hot

حار

#834
loud

عالي

#835
sea

بحر

#836
volcano

بركان

#837
steam

بخار

#838

rainbow

قوس قزح

#839

dawn

فجر

#840

rain

مطر

#841

wave

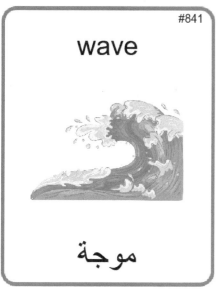

موجة

#842

stormy

عاصف

#843

wet

مبتل

#844

climate

مناخ

#845

moon

قمر

#846

cloudy

غائم

#847
rainy

ممطر

#848
sunny

مشمس

#849
location

موقع

#850
summer

صيف

#851
snow

ثلج

#852
quiet

هادئ

#853
disaster

كارثة

#854
earth

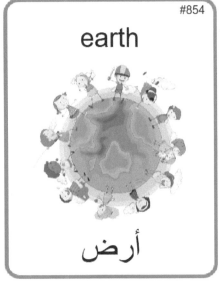

أرض

#855
foggy

ضبابي

#856
month

شهر

#857
morning

صباح

#858
autumn

خريف

#859
date

تاريخ

#860
noon

ظهر

#861
day

يوم

#862
week

أسبوع

#863
midnight

منتصف الليل

#864
night

ليل

#865
time

وقت

#866
year

سنة

#867
song

أغنية

#868
industry

صناعة

#869
ice

ثلج

#870
movie

فيلم

#871
war

حرب

#872
arrow

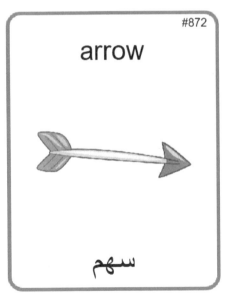

سهم

#873
winner

فائز

#874
game

لعبة

#875
homework

واجب منزلي

#876
sculpture

تمثال

#877
octagon

مثمن

#878
law

قانون

#879
language

لغة

#880
wheel
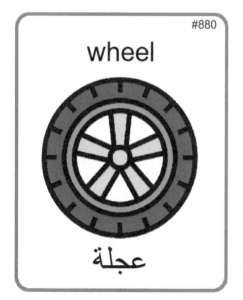
عجلة

#881
cube
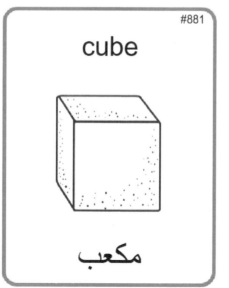
مكعب

#882
product

منتج

#883
art

فن

#884
birthday

عيد ميلاد

#885
chemistry

كيمياء

#886
government

حكومة

#887
disease

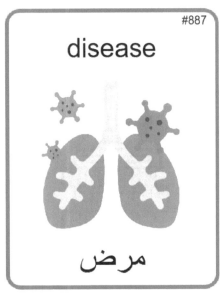

مرض

#888
bubble

فقاعة

#889
package

طرود

#890
country

بلد

#891
painting

لوحة

#892
income

دخل

#893
point

نقطة

#894
user

مستخدم

#895
triangle

مثلث

#896
scale
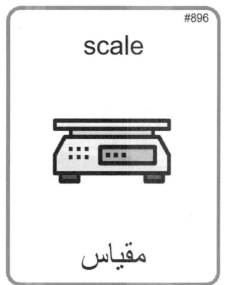
مقياس

#897
passenger

راكب

#898
math

رياضيات

#899
fire

نار

#900
wedding

زفاف

#901
paint

طلاء

#902
debt

دين

#903
dirt

أوساخ

#904
story

قصة

#905
error

خطأ

#906
worker

عامل

#907
square
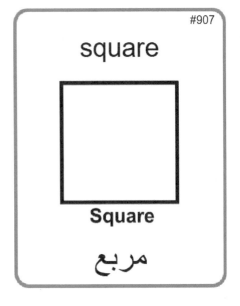
Square
مربع

#908
signature

توقيع

#909
message

رسالة

#910
christmas

عيد الميلاد

#911
pair

زوج

#912
customer

زبون

#913
news

أخبار

#914
circle
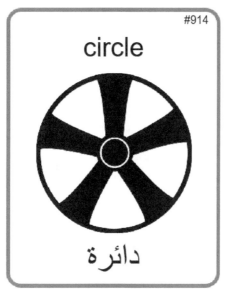
دائرة

#915
funeral

جنازة

#916
number

رقم

#917
company

شركة

#918
cafe

مقهى

#919
airport

مطار

#920
lighthouse

منارة

#921
school

مدرسة

#922
jungle

غابة

#923
library

مكتبة

#924
grocery

بقالة

#925
market

سوق

#926
hill

تلة

#927
apartment

شقة

#928
desert

صحراء

#929
island

جزيرة

#930
dam
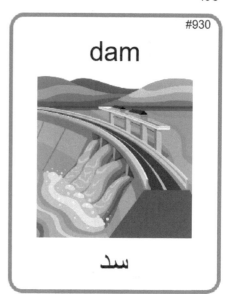
سد

#931
university

جامعة

#932
city

مدينة

#933
shop

متجر

#934
hospital

مستشفى

#935
village

قرية

#936
highway

طريق سريع

#937
factory

مصنع

#938
classroom

فصل دراسي

#939
supermarket

سوبر ماركت

#940
lab

مختبر

#941
estate

عقارات

#942
beach

شاطئ

#943
town

بلدة

#944
joyful

مبتهج

#945
delicious

لذيذ

#946
up

أعلى

#947
sleepy

نعسان

#948
fat

سمين

#949
cute

لطيف

#950
scary

مخيف

#951
under

تحت

#952
sad

حزين

#953
bad

سيئ

#954
shy

خجول

#955
big

كبير

#956
stack

كومة

#957
smelling

رائحة

#958
aggressive

عدواني

#959
impress

إعجاب

#960
stinky

كريه الرائحة

#961
strong

قوي

#962
unhappy

حزين

#963
stylish

أنيق

#964
friendly

ودود

#965
pretty

جميل

#966
mad

غاضب

#967
fresh

طازج

#968
bored

ضجر

#969
happy

سعيد

#970
good

جيد

#971
proud

فخور

#972
data

بيانات

#973
activity

نشاط

#974
fact

حقيقة

#975
revenue

إيرادات

#976
evil

شر

#977
goal

هدف

#978
exam

امتحان

#979
health

صحة

#980
technology

تكنولوجيا

#981
freedom

حرية

#982
society

مجتمع

#983
anxiety

قلق

#984
profit

ربح

#985
investment

استثمار

#986
history

تاريخ

#987
wealth

ثروة

#988
knowledge

معرفة

#989
entertainment

ترفيه

#990
theory
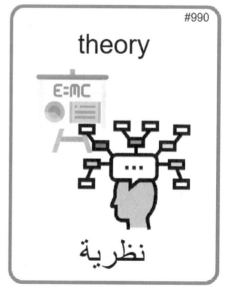
نظرية

#991
education

تعليم

#992
economics

اقتصاديات

#993
energy

طاقة

#994
question

سؤال

#995
direction
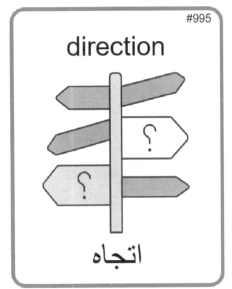
اتجاه

#996
safety

سلامة

#997
friendship

صداقة

#998
ability

قدرة

#999
idea

فكرة

#1000

security

أمن